Helen Keller

Helen Keller

⠠⠓⠑⠇⠑⠝ ⠠⠅⠑⠇⠇⠑⠗

HER LIFE IN PICTURES

GEORGE SULLIVAN

Foreword by
Keller Johnson Thompson

SCHOLASTIC INC.

Braille letters and numbers in this book are set in simulated braille (simbraille), a type of braille using shadow dots. Simbraille uses a print representation of braille characters to aid sighted persons in reading the letters, numbers, and punctuation marks of standard braille.

a	b	c	d	e	f	g	h	i	j	k	l	m

n	o	p	q	r	s	t	u	v	w	x	y	z

Capital Sign	Number Sign	Period	Comma	Question Mark	Semi-colon	Exclamation Point	Opening Quote	Closing Quote

1 •• 4 The six dots of the braille
2 •• 5 cell are arranged and
3 •• 6 numbered 1 through 6.

• • The capital sign, dot 6,
• • placed before a letter
• • makes a capital letter.

• • The number sign, dots 3, 4, 5, 6,
• • placed before the characters a through
• • j makes the numbers 1 through 0.

Acknowledgments

A good number of individuals and organizations were helpful to me in providing the background information and photographs used in this book, and I am grateful to each of them. Special thanks are due to: Helen Selsdon, Archivist, and Alina Vayntrub, American Foundation for the Blind; Barbara Castleman and Stephanie Sullivan, Perkins School for the Blind; Sue Pilkilton, Ivy Green; Faye Haskins, Martin Luther King Memorial Library; Ann M. Shumard, National Portrait Gallery; Jennifer S. Klopp, Helen Keller International; Pamela Reed Sanchez, George Eastman House, International Museum of Photography and Film; Lois Bloom, Historical Society of Easton, Connecticut; Greg Rixon, Washington National Cathedral; photo researcher Athena Angelos, Washington, D.C., and Sal Alberti and James Lowe, James Lowe Autographs.   — GEORGE SULLIVAN, New York City

Book design by Nancy Sabato. Cover design by Becky Terhune.
Cover photograph courtesy the Library of Congress.

ISBN-13: 978-0-545-68531-3   ISBN-10: 0-545-68531-1

10 11 12 13 14 15 16 17 18 19   40   28 27 26 25 24 23 22 21 20 19

Scholastic Inc., 557 Broadway, New York, NY 10012

Contents

Foreword

I remember the day vividly. It was the fall of 1979, and my grandmother, Patty Tyson Johnson, Helen Keller's niece, had just granted me an interview. I wanted to talk to her about the life and legacy of Helen Keller for my fourth-grade history project. As Grandmother relayed story after story of her visits with the world-famous Helen Keller, I was quite taken with this deaf and blind woman's life, and was amazed at her incredible accomplishments.

As a nine-year-old child growing up in Helen Keller's hometown of Tuscumbia, Alabama, I always presumed that the miraculous story of Helen Keller's life ended when at the age of seven, her teacher, Anne Sullivan, broke through her dark and silent world by teaching her that everything in the world had a name, using finger spelling and an old water pump. My grandmother patiently explained that this was only the beginning of Helen Keller's life. Her personal victory over darkness and silence turned Helen's life and her ambitions to the service of others. With much excitement and determination, she dedicated her life to helping others by speaking, writing, traveling, and working constantly to improve the lives of deaf and blind people throughout the world.

It has been more than twenty years since that fateful fall day—the day that I would not only better understand the life of my great-grandaunt Helen, but a day that would change the course of my own life forever. For on that day, I vowed to follow in my aunt Helen's footsteps and make a difference in the world around me. Today, I am the Ambassador for the American Foundation for the Blind, and Vice-President of Education at the Helen Keller Foundation, but every day, I am inspired by Helen Keller.

Helen Keller once said, "Life is either a daring adventure, or nothing at all." For me, thanks to the life and legacy of Helen Keller, it has been such an adventure.

KELLER JOHNSON THOMPSON
Great-grandniece of Helen Keller

Helen with Annie Sullivan in 1914. Helen was 34, Annie was 48.

Introduction

Helen Keller holds a special place among American heroes. No one else is quite like her. She could not hear. She could not see. When she spoke, she could barely be understood. Yet she learned to live and express her thoughts and feelings in a world of sight and sound. She showed that the disabled, as she put it, could "live naturally and...be treated as human beings." Through her courage and strength, she brought hope to both the blind and the seeing.

Helen visited Japan in 1947. In remote towns and villages, crowds greeted her by shouting her name, "Helen Keller! Helen Keller!" Before television and cell phones, Helen Keller was known on every continent.

Helen Keller's story is known to millions. She was born in Tuscumbia, Alabama, on June 27, 1880. When she was nineteen months old, she developed what the family doctor called "brain fever." The disease might have been scarlet fever or meningitis, an inflammation of the brain and spinal cord. Whatever it might have been, there were no medicines available at that time to treat it. After a few days, the terrible fever left her and she fell into a deep sleep. Once she awakened, it did not take her mother long to realize that her daughter could not hear or see. Helen would live in silence and darkness for the rest of her life.

In her early years, the deaf-blind child was wild and would not obey. Her parents did not know what to do. Change came on a March day in 1887, a few months before Helen's seventh birthday. Annie Sullivan arrived at the Keller home to be Helen's teacher. In the months that followed, Helen was changed forever. By spelling out words in Helen's hand, Annie was able to "speak" to the deaf-blind girl. She inspired Helen to read and study. She succeeded in opening Helen's mind.

As a little girl, Helen said, "Someday I shall go to college." And she did. She entered Radcliffe College in Cambridge, Massachusetts, in 1900. Annie Sullivan

Helen enjoys a game of chess with Annie Sullivan. At the time, Helen was a student at Radcliffe College.

went with her, tapping out lectures and books into Helen's hand. After graduating from college, Helen became active on behalf of the blind and deaf-blind. She wrote articles and books. She gave lectures. She helped to raise many millions of dollars for organizations that aided the blind.

Helen Keller loved to travel. Her efforts to improve conditions for the blind and deaf-blind took her to every corner of the globe. From 1901 to 1957, Helen visited thirty-nine countries on six continents.

The blind and deaf-blind were always Helen's chief mission. But she was also a fiery social critic. She supported the right of workers to strike and form unions. She joined the millions of women who sought to gain the legal power to vote in political elections. She even favored such extreme measures as hunger strikes and smashing windows in support of that cause.

Helen Keller hated war. Instead, she said, nations should fight for "liberty, justice, and an abundant life for all." In 1917, the United States prepared to enter World War I. Helen loudly opposed the move. She said it "means death and misery to millions of human beings."

Helen Keller belonged to an earlier time. In recent decades, her fame has faded. Yet millions today benefit from her lifework. Her chief message was: "We're like everybody else. We're here to be able to live a life as full as a sighted person's. And it's O.K. to be ourselves." Those words meant that the blind and deaf-blind—any disabled person, in fact—could lead an independent life. It meant that they had the freedom to be exceptional, even amazing. It meant they could be like Helen Keller herself.

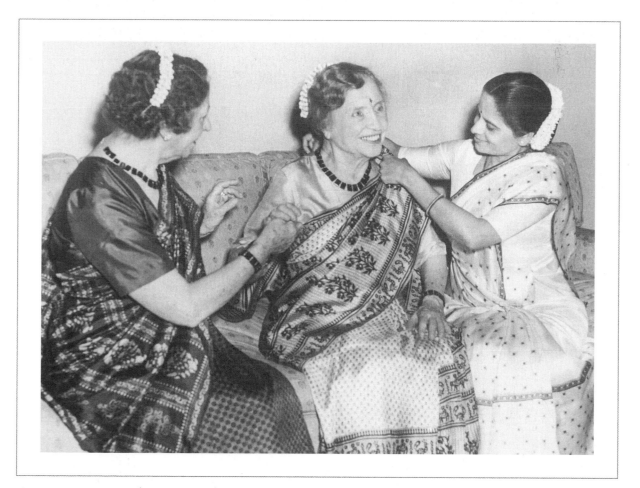

On a visit to Bombay (now Mumbai), India, in 1955, Helen gets a helping hand in the arrangement of her sari.

Her Life in Pictures

*H*elen Keller never saw her own face in a mirror. Yet how she looked was important to her. Her hair was smartly styled. What she wore was well chosen. She could flash a winning smile—when it was called for. Pictures of her gave no clue that she was blind and deaf. Nor did people realize that, as an adult, she had her eyes surgically removed and replaced with ones made of blue glass. "I want all the handicapped to look nice," she once told a friend. Throughout her long life, Helen Keller worked hard to improve the lives of others. Always looking good was part of the struggle.

Helen's father, Captain Arthur Keller, served proudly in the Confederate Army during the Civil War. The family income came from the small farm he owned. Helen's mother, Kate Adams, was twenty-two when she married the forty-two-year-old widower. While she had servants to help her run the farm, she raised her own fruit, vegetables, and farm animals, including chickens, turkeys, sheep, and pigs. She also made her own butter, lard, ham, and bacon. She was especially proud of her flower garden, where she grew roses of great beauty.

The Keller homestead in Tuscumbia, Alabama, was called "Ivy Green."
The name came from the English ivy that wound about the house, cottage,
nearby fences, and trees. The main house (top) had four large rooms on the
first floor. Each room had a fireplace.

The Keller estate also included a cottage that was east of the main house,
known as "The Little House" (below). It had one large room and a smaller
one. Honeybees and hummingbirds regularly visited its yellow roses and
honeysuckle. Helen was born in the cottage.
She lived there with a nurse until she
became sick, and then later with her
first teacher, Annie Sullivan.

⠆⠒ *T*his is one of the first photographs taken of Helen. By this time in her life, she knew she was different from other people. They spoke with their mouths. Being deaf and blind, Helen could not. She got angry as a result. She cried, kicked, and screamed. Her parents were unable to control her.

*A*fter Helen was born, the Kellers had two other children. (They are pictured here with their nurse.) Her sister, Mildred (right), was five years younger than Helen. Her brother, Phillips, was the baby of the family. Helen was almost twelve when Phillips was born.

ℋelen's mother and father knew that Helen needed help. Mrs. Keller recalled reading about Laura Bridgman. Laura was blind and deaf but had been educated at the Perkins Institution for the Blind in Boston (below), which was the first school in America for the blind and deaf-blind. This postcard photograph dates to the early 1890s. Captain Keller wrote to the school. He asked for a teacher who could come to the Keller home to work with Helen.

ichael Anagnos, the head of the Perkins school, wrote back to Captain Keller. He named one of the school's recent graduates and its valedictorian as the person for the job. Her name was Annie Sullivan. She was twenty years old. Anagnos said she was "intelligent, strictly honest, [and] ladylike." When the job as Helen's teacher was offered to her, Annie accepted it.

At first, Annie could not control Helen and her quick temper. She absolutely refused to obey and sometimes raged like a wild animal. But Annie was able to change her into a manageable child. "She lets me kiss her now," said Annie in a letter to Michael Anagnos. "And when she is in a particularly gentle mood, she will sit in my lap for a minute or two." When Annie began teaching Helen a finger alphabet, she first put a doll in Helen's arms. Then she took one of Helen's hands and spelled out the shapes of the letters d - o - l - l in her palm. With Helen's other hand, she stroked the doll. Helen quickly learned to spell out the letters in Annie's palm. But the word she was spelling meant nothing to her. She did not connect it to the object itself.

One day, Helen and Annie were together at the water pump behind the Keller home. Annie took one of Helen's hands and placed it in the cool flow of water. In the palm of the other hand, she spelled out w - a - t - e - r. Instantly, Helen's face brightened. "Suddenly, I felt [as if] somehow the mystery of language was revealed to me. I knew then that 'w - a - t - e - r' meant the wonderful cool something that was flowing over my hand."

By the end of her first year with Annie, Helen was a good reader. She learned to read books with raised printing and was introduced to braille, a system of reading and writing for the blind. Groups of raised dots represent letters and numbers. A blind person reads by running his or her fingertips over the dots.

23

Helen also learned how to write by forming squarish letters on paper with a pencil. She first placed a ruler on the page and used it as a guide. Helen liked to write letters. She sometimes ended her letters with this phrase: "I am too tired to write more." She also wrote some letters in braille.

Helen, accompanied by Annie Sullivan, began attending the Perkins Institution for the Blind in May 1888. Helen was delighted to meet the school's students. They could "spell with their fingers," she said. At the time, the school had one of the largest collections of books with raised printing in the world. It thrilled Helen to be able to read so many books. Here, Helen (seated) poses with one of the school's young students.

*W*orking with Annie Sullivan, Helen also learned to read lips. She did so by feeling the vibration of the words being spoken. She placed her middle finger on the speaker's nose. She put her forefinger on the lips. She rested her thumb on the larynx. She could then understand what the speaker was saying.

As a teenager, Helen was praised for her loveliness. She sometimes posed for studio photographs meant to show off her good looks.
She was thirteen in this photograph. It was said to reveal her beauty, purity, and kindliness.

*I*t upset Helen that she could not speak well. In the fall of 1894, she entered the Wright-Humason School for the Deaf in New York City. She hoped the school would make her speech normal. But her ability to speak did not improve. The school was a disappointment to her. Here, Helen appears in her graduation picture, taken in 1895. She is at the far left, seated, holding Annie's hand.

⠃ While in New York City, Helen and Annie made many new friends. One was Mark Twain, the most famous American writer of the time. He looked upon Helen as the most remarkable woman he had ever met. He had high praise for Annie, too. For her work with Helen, he called Annie a "miracle worker."

⠃ Alexander Graham Bell, the inventor of the telephone, was another of Helen's admirers. Bell had a lifelong interest in teaching the deaf. He and Helen wrote to each other frequently. Helen often signed her letters, "Your loving little friend." Here, Helen (left) and Bell are pictured with Annie Sullivan.

⠠⠓elen dreamed of going to college. But at the time, college was mostly for the sons of rich families. Few young women continued their education beyond high school. But Helen was determined. She eventually applied and was admitted to Radcliffe College, a college for women in Cambridge, Massachusetts.

At Radcliffe, Helen was sometimes lonely. Only one of the other students knew the finger alphabet. That made it difficult for Helen to make friends. Her classmates understood how she felt. To show their friendship, they bought her this Boston terrier. Helen named the dog Phiz.

ℋelen studied French, German, Latin, history, and English composition and literature in college. But only a handful of the books were printed for the blind. Annie spent hours each day spelling books into Helen's hand word by word.

$\therefore$ $\mathcal{A}$t Radcliffe, Helen's writing skills grew. She used a typewriter with a braille keyboard. She wrote articles about her life and world that appeared in *Ladies' Home Journal*, a national magazine. Eventually, the articles became a book titled *The Story of My Life*. Published in 1903, the book brought Helen even greater fame.

𝓘n the fall of 1904. Helen graduated from Radcliffe. Her diploma bore the Latin words *cum laude*, meaning "with honor." In praise of her feat, her classmates composed this poem for the yearbook. It read:

> *Beside her task our efforts pale,*
> *She never knew the word for fail;*
> *Beside her triumph ours are naught,*
> *For hers were far more dearly bought.*

After Helen's graduation from Radcliffe, she and Annie moved into this big house they had bought in the spring in Wrentham, Massachusetts. It had seventeen rooms. (In this photograph, the house is decorated for the Fourth of July.) During one summer there, Helen described the house in a letter to a friend. She said, "It is old-fashioned, roomy and cheerful. I never had a room for all my books before." One of her favorite spots on the property was by an old stone wall. Tall pines and spruces stood near the wall. "I can walk alone there," Helen said in her letter, "and feel rich in having this space to myself."

Much of Helen's world was now based on her keen sense of touch. This ability enabled her to "hear" music. She enjoyed the organ the most. She could touch it and sense its vibrations. The violin was another instrument that delighted her. She found its notes to be more delicate than those of the organ.

⠠⠹ Through her sense of touch, Helen was able to identify the faces of friends. She could admire famous works of sculpture and enjoy being outdoors. As she put it, she was able to appreciate "the delicate shapes of flowers, the noble forms of trees, and the range of mighty winds."

While at Radcliffe, Helen and Annie met John Macy. He was an English instructor at Harvard. He was young, bright, and charming. John and Annie fell in love. In May 1905, the two were married. John was twenty-eight. Annie was thirty-nine. Afterward, John, Annie, and Helen lived together at the house in Wrentham. Helen often said that John was like "a brother" to her. She kept busy writing articles and books, with John taking on the role of her editor. Helen's writing improved as a result. In a sculpted portrait of her that dates to this period (right), Helen is quoted as follows: "To be blind is to see the bright side of life."

The First Appearance on the Lecture Platform of

HELEN KELLER
And her Teacher Mrs. Macy (Anne M. Sullivan)

SUBJECT

"The Heart and the Hand," or the Right Use of our Senses

TREMONT TEMPLE, Boston
ONE NIGHT ONLY
MONDAY EVENING, MARCH 24th, at 8:15 P. M.
SEATS, 25c. to $1.50. NOW ON SALE

Approaching her mid-thirties, Helen decided to become a lecturer. She would give planned talks. Audiences would pay to hear her. But her voice was a problem. It had a hollow sound like that of a robot. In her first try as a lecturer, her voice was unclear, and she knew it. She left the stage in tears. But Helen would not give up. She kept trying and, before long, she was able to amaze and inspire an audience.

After the United States entered World War I in 1917, Helen spent time with American soldiers who had been blinded in the conflict. Such visits sometimes made her feel "useless." Some people were always eager for war, she realized. When they got what they wanted, it quickly led to more men and women becoming wounded and blinded.

In 1918, Helen went to Hollywood to star in a silent movie about her life, *Deliverance*. She was seen reading braille, playing the trumpet, and strolling through her garden. She even flew in an old biplane. In the photograph at the right, Helen is seated between Annie Sullivan and Polly Thomson. Comic film actor Charlie Chaplin is standing. Polly had been hired as a secretary and an assistant for Helen and Annie in 1914. Helen was never very fond of *Deliverance*. Nor was the public. The film was a failure at the box office.

The 8th Wonder of the World
Helen Keller
IN THE PHOTO-PLAY BEAUTIFUL
"DELIVERANCE"

TOGETHER WITH HER LIFE LONG FRIEND, COMPANION and BELOVED INSTRUCTOR ANNE SULLIVAN (MACY) BOTH APPEARING PERSONALLY IN THIS MOST INTERESTING and INCOMPARABLE OF PHOTO-PLAYS

DIRECT FROM HER TRIUMPHANT TOUR OF AMERICA'S BEST THEATRES

TREMONT TEMPLE | Commencing Mon. Eve | JULY 19

LIBBIE PRINTING COMPANY 242 DOVER ST., BOSTON

⠆⠆ *H*elen loved to ride. In this photograph, taken in Beverly Hills, California, in 1919, she appears confident as a rider. Helen, however, never set out on horseback by herself. Polly or another friend rode with her, holding a lead rein.

During the early 1920s, Helen and Annie traveled the country as vaudeville performers, sometimes earning as much as two thousand dollars a week. Helen delighted in the "rush, glare, and noise" of the theater. Annie would open their twenty-minute act by telling about Helen's life. Then Helen would speak and take questions from the audience. "Who are the most unhappy people?" Helen was once asked. "People who have nothing to do," she answered.

elen and Annie traveled to Europe in 1931. Paris was one of their stops. While there, Helen (third from the left) visited French soldiers who had been blinded during World War I. She also gave money to aid blinded German soldiers. Germany had fought against France during the war. Helen thus was criticized. She protested. She had not "taken sides," she said. She was "neutral."

𝒯he U.S. government held a World Conference on Work for the Blind in April 1931 in New York City. The American Foundation for the Blind and Helen helped to organize the event. Some one hundred and ten people from thirty-two countries took part. After the conference, President Herbert Hoover met with the delegates at the White House. (President Hoover is at the center of this photograph; Helen is at his right.)

$\mathcal{T}$his is one of the last photographs taken of Helen and Annie together. (Helen is standing between Annie, on the left, and Polly, on the right.) Annie died in 1936 after a long illness. In Annie's final moments, Helen was at her bedside holding her hand. Grief-stricken,

DOCTORS HOSPITAL

EAST END AVE. AT 87TH ST.

NEW YORK

> For fifty years Anne Sullivan
> Macy, my beloved teacher, has been the
> light in my life. Now she is ill and the
> darkness that covers me has fallen upon
> her; still the light of her love shines
> amid the encircling gloom, and we are
> happy.
>
> Helen Heller

Helen felt "a loneliness…that will always be immense," but she realized that she had work to do for the blind and deaf-blind. That, and her belief in an afterlife, gave her strength. (Above, a letter that Helen wrote during Annie's illness.)

After Annie Sullivan's passing, Helen came to depend more on Polly Thomson. Like others close to Helen, Polly used the finger alphabet to "speak" with Helen. Polly, a loyal Scotswoman, would be at Helen's side for almost thirty years.

𝓑eginning in the early 1940s, Helen enjoyed a close friendship with sculptor Jo Davidson and his wife, Florence. When Helen spoke out on political matters, Davidson encouraged her. In the presidential election of 1944, Helen and Davidson actively supported Franklin Delano Roosevelt.

A big white house in Easton, Connecticut, became home to Helen and Polly in September 1939. Roomy and comfortable, it was surrounded by woods and meadows. They named it Arcan Ridge. A rail fence made it possible for Helen to make her way about the property by herself.

On summer mornings, she would get up at five o'clock
to tend her flowers. By touch, she could tell the
flowers from the weeds. Fire destroyed the house in
November 1946 while Helen and Polly were in Rome.
The house pictured at left replaced it—it was almost
identical to the original one.

During World War II, Helen wished to "see" one of the Army Air Force's huge B-17 "Flying Fortress" bombers close up. Her chance came in September 1943 when she visited the plant in Seattle, Washington, where the plane was made. Here, Helen inspects a pair of machine guns with which the plane was equipped.

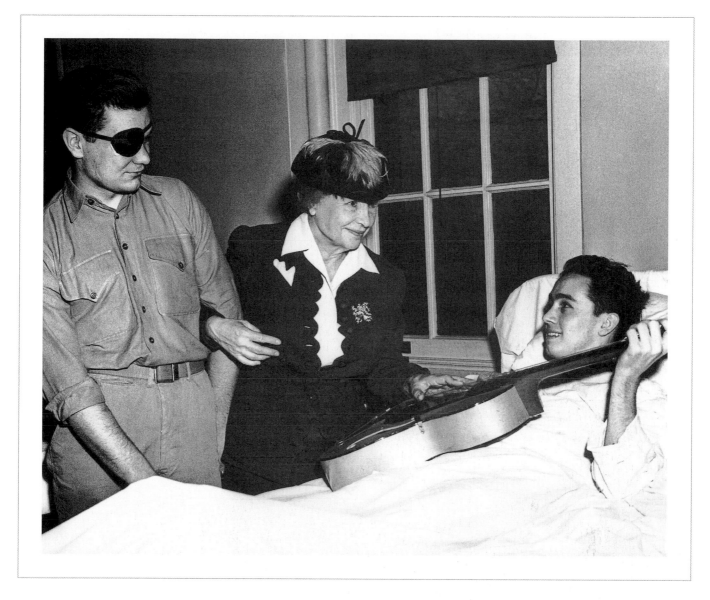

⠃ *H*elen often visited the wounded in military hospitals during and after World War II. The men and women were happy to see her. They were also surprised. They had read articles about her. They had heard about Helen from their parents. To them, Helen was a legend.

⠿ *F*rom 1946 to 1957, Helen and Polly traveled almost without
letup. In 1946, at an institution in Rome, Helen visited young
children who had been blinded or crippled during World War II.
The nun pictured here wears a traditional habit.

$\mathcal{I}$n 1948, Helen and Polly set out on a long trip to Australia, New Zealand, and Japan. Helen was sixty-eight. "How do you approach old age?" a student asked her. "There's no age to the spirit," Helen said. Here, in Australia, Helen is almost buried by young fans.

When Helen and Polly were in Japan in 1948, big crowds turned out to see and hear them. In Tokyo, Helen spoke outside the Imperial Palace. There she attracted this huge throng, numbering in the tens of thousands.

While in Japan, Helen and Polly went to Hiroshima and Nagasaki. Toward the end of World War II, both cities had been the targets of the United States' atomic bombs. Hiroshima was completely leveled; Nagasaki was devastated. More than two hundred thousand people died instantly. In Hiroshima (above), Polly described the scene to Helen. Helen became even more determined to fight against "the demons of atomic warfare and for peace."

*I*n the election for president in 1948, Helen backed Henry Wallace. At the time, there was a growing fear of Communism in the United States, and Wallace was known for being a left-wing Democrat. Helen's closeness to Wallace upset Helen's friends. They feared her friendship with him could cause harm to her good name.

⠃ *T*he United Nations was formed in 1945. From the very first, Helen supported the U.N. and its goal of world peace. Here, she meets a member of the U.N. Secretariat from India in 1949. Polly Thomson (behind Helen) looks on. At the time, the U.N. was based at a temporary site in Lake Success, New York.

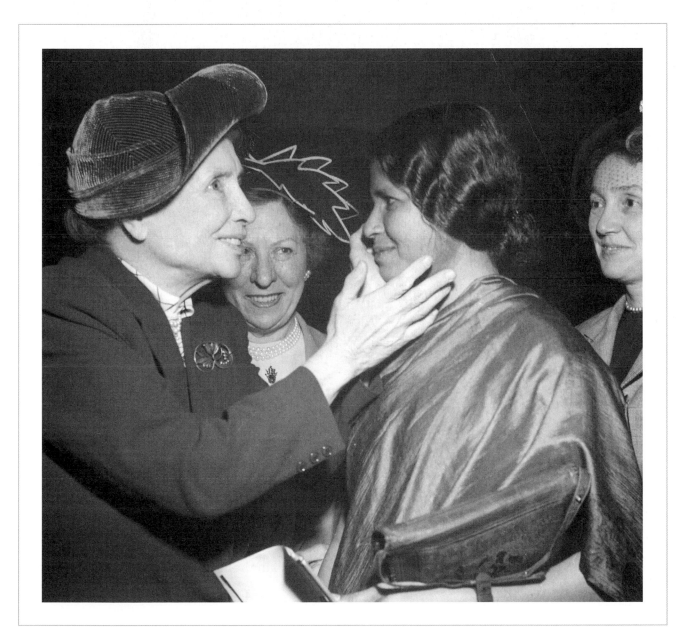

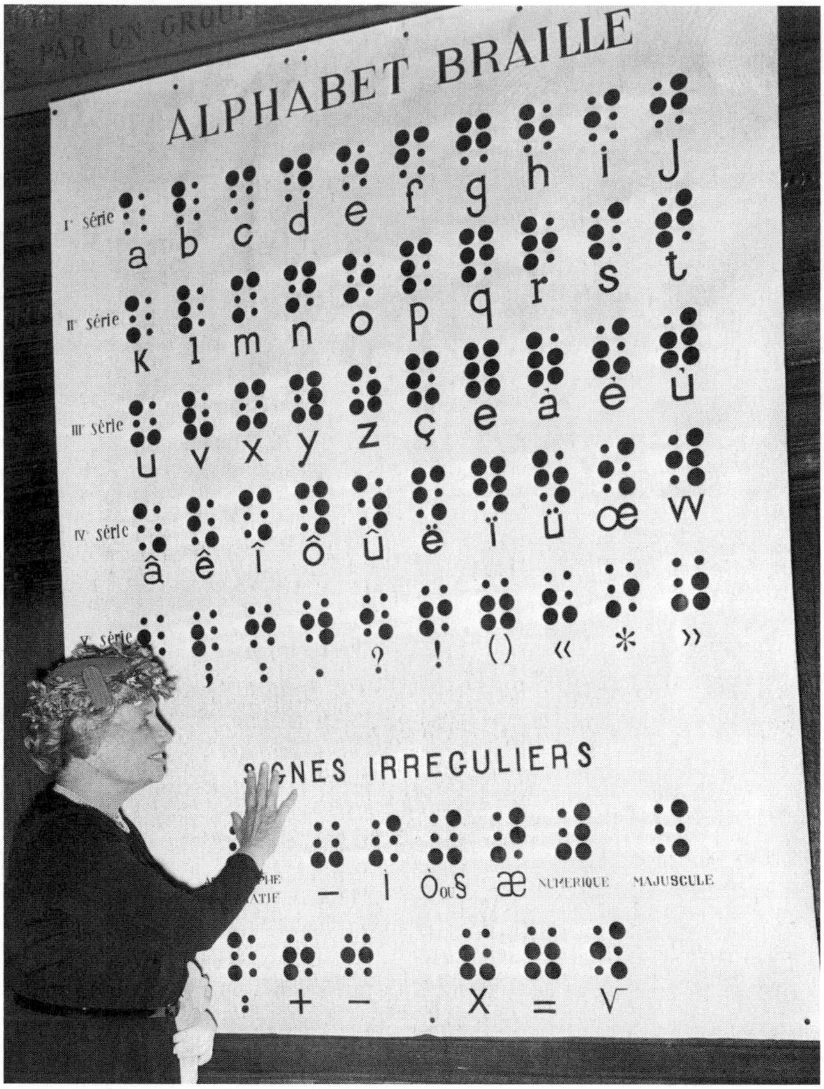

A Frenchman who lost his sight at age three, Louis Braille (1809-1852) invented the worldwide system for reading and writing used by the blind, now known as braille. On the one hundredth anniversary of his death, Helen gave a speech in Paris at the ceremonies held in his honor (pictured here). "We the blind," she said, "are as indebted to Louis Braille as mankind is to Gutenberg."

⠃⠃ *H*elen and Polly Thomson met President Dwight D. Eisenhower at the White House early in November 1953. Helen said she wished to "see" the president's famed smile. After being introduced, she touched the president's face for a brief moment. An alert photographer made this picture. It appeared in newspapers in every part of the country.

Helen and Eleanor Roosevelt, the wife of President Franklin Delano Roosevelt, were close friends for many years. Mrs. Roosevelt saw in Helen someone with the same spirit as her husband. President Roosevelt, crippled by polio at age thirty-nine, had conquered his disability. "Franklin's illness...gave him strength and courage he had not had before," Mrs. Roosevelt said.

When Helen visited India in 1955, she received a warm welcome from Jawaharlal Nehru, the nation's prime minister. It was the high point of her trip. Nehru permitted Helen to touch his face. She said it had "real nobility."

The Unconquered, a documentary about Helen's life, was released in 1954. The film featured a dance especially choreographed for Helen by Martha Graham, the world famous dancer and choreographer. In this photograph, Helen, assisted by Graham (at Helen's right), is "feeling" the dance, raising her arms high and moving easily to its rhythm.

𝒪n June 27, 1955, at Arcan Ridge, Helen celebrated her seventy-fifth birthday. Polly Thomson helped her cut the cake. At this stage of her life, Helen was often being hailed as the greatest living American woman.

The Miracle Worker made Helen even more famous. The hit play opened in New York on October 19, 1959, and told of Annie Sullivan's early success as Helen's teacher. Anne Bancroft was cast as Annie Sullivan; Patty Duke played Helen as a child (left). The actresses recreated their roles when *The Miracle Worker* was made into a movie in 1962, and both won Academy Awards. (Below, Helen meets Patty Duke at Helen's eightieth birthday celebration in New York.)

Polly Thomson died in 1960. Afterward, Helen cut back on her work schedule. There was one event she did not want to miss, however. That was her 1961 visit with President John F. Kennedy in the White House. Evelyn Seide is at Helen's side. Evelyn now managed the Keller household at Arcan Ridge.

$\therefore$ $\mathcal{N}$ow in her eighties, Helen had little interest in being the public person she once was. She spent more time with her family and friends. One winter, she stayed with her brother Phillips in Dallas. She enjoyed visits from her sister Mildred. (Above, Helen rests at her home in Connecticut.) Helen died in 1968.

After Helen's passing, the burial urn containing her ashes was placed next to Annie's and Polly's at the National Cathedral in Washington, D.C. A small block of stone sculpted in her image, called a corbel, projects from one of the cathedral's stone walls.

⠃ Through her long life, Helen Keller worked to change the lives of the blind and deaf-blind. And she succeeded. Today, work in her name is being carried on in every part of the world. Here, in Tanzania, a young boy's eyes are examined by a doctor who represents Helen Keller International. The organization is devoted to fighting blindness and malnutrition. It operates in twenty-one countries.

Chronology

1880 · (June 27) Helen Keller born in Tuscumbia, Alabama.

1882 · Keller loses sight, hearing, and power of speech.

1887 · Annie Sullivan arrives in Tuscumbia to be Keller's teacher.

1888 · Keller visits Perkins Institution for the Blind in Boston.

1891 · Keller writes the short story "The Frost King."

1894 · Keller enters Wright-Humason School in New York City.

1896 · Keller enters Cambridge School for Young Ladies.

1900 · Keller enters Radcliffe College in Boston.

1902–1903 · Keller's *The Story of My Life* is published.

1904 · Keller graduates from Radcliffe.

1905 · Annie Sullivan marries John Macy.

1908 · Keller's *The World I Live In* is published.

1909 · Keller becomes a member of the Socialist Party.

1913 · Keller's *Out of the Dark* is published.

1914 · Polly Thomson joins the Keller household as a secretary and assistant.

1916 · Keller meets Peter Fagan, an associate of John Macy's; the two make
marriage plans that are never carried out.

1919 · Keller stars in the film *Deliverance*.

1920 · Keller begins a career in vaudeville with Annie Sullivan Macy.

1924 · Keller begins work with the American Foundation for the Blind.

1927 · Keller's *My Religion* is published.

1929 · Keller's *Midstream* is published.

1936 · Annie Sullivan Macy dies.

1937 · Keller tours Japan, Korea, and Manchuria with Polly Thomson.

1938 · Keller's *Journal* is published.

1954 · Ivy Green, Keller's home in Tuscumbia, Alabama, is listed on the National Register of Historic Places.

1955 · *Teacher: Anne Sullivan Macy* is published.

1956 · *The Unconquered*, a documentary film based on Keller's life (later renamed *Helen Keller in Her Story*) wins an Academy Award.

1957 · *The Miracle Worker* is first performed on television.

1959 · *The Miracle Worker* opens on Broadway.

1960 · Polly Thomson dies.

1962 · Film version of *The Miracle Worker* is released; Anne Bancroft (in the role of Annie Sullivan) and Patty Duke (as Helen Keller) win Academy Awards in 1963.

1964 · Keller receives the Presidential Medal of Freedom, the nation's highest civilian award, from President Lyndon Baines Johnson.

1968 · (June 1) Helen Keller dies at Arcan Ridge, her home in Connecticut.

Bibliography

Hermann, Dorothy. *Helen Keller: A Life.* New York: Alfred A. Knopf, 1998.

Keller, Helen. *Midstream: My Later Life.* New York: Doubleday, Doran, 1938.

_____. *Out of the Dark.* New York: Doubleday, 1913.

_____. *The Story of My Life.* New York: Bantam Classic, 2005.

_____. *Teacher: Anne Sullivan Macy.* New York: Doubleday, 1955.

_____. *The World I Live In.* New York: New York Review of Books, 2003.

Lash, Joseph. *Helen and Teacher: The Story of Helen Keller and Anne Sullivan Macy.* New York: Addison-Wesley. 1997.

Further Reading

Dash, Joan. *The World at Her Fingertips: The Story of Helen Keller.* New York: Scholastic, 2002.

Davidson, Margaret. *Helen Keller.* New York: Scholastic, 1997.

_____. *Helen Keller's Teacher.* New York: Scholastic, 1992.

Keller, Helen. *To Love This Life*: *Quotations by Helen Keller.* New York: AFB Press, 2000.

Lawler, Laurie. *Helen Keller: Rebellious Spirit.* New York: Holiday House, 2001.

Lundell, Margo. *Una Niña Llamada Helen Keller.* New York: Scholastic en Español, 2003.

Nicholson, Lois. *Helen Keller: Humanitarian.* New York: Chelsea House, 1996.

Sullivan, George. *In Their Own Words: Helen Keller.* New York: Scholastic, 2000.

For More Information

American Foundation for the Blind
11 Penn Plaza
New York, NY 10001
Web site: www.afb.org

The Canadian Helen Keller Centre, Inc.
210 Empress Avenue
Toronto, ON M2N 3T9
Web site: www.chkc.org

Helen Keller International
352 Park Avenue South
Suite 100
New York, NY 10010
Web site: www.hki.org

Helen Keller National Center
  for Deaf-Blind Youths and Adults
III Middle Neck Road
Sands Point, NY 11050
Web site: www.helenkeller.org/national

Ivy Green (Birthplace of Helen Keller)
300 North Commons
Tuscumbia, AL 35674
Web site: www.bham.net/Keller/home.htm

Perkins School for the Blind
175 North Beacon Street
Watertown, MA 02172
Web site: www.perkins.org

Ask Keller

Keller Johnson Thompson is Helen Keller's great-grandniece. From her home
in Tuscumbia, Alabama, she will answer your questions about Helen Keller's life.
Here is her Web site: www.afb.org/braillebug/askkeller.asp

Photo Credits

Photos ©: American Foundation for the Blind: 6, 10, 13, 19, 20, 21, 22, 23, 24, 26,
27, 28, 30, 31, 34, 35, 36, 37, 40 center left, 41 center left, 42, 43, 44, 45, 46, 47,
48, 49, 51, 54, 55, 58, 59, 60, 61, 62, 63, 65, 66, 68, 69, 71, 72; AP Images: 53 (Sam
Myers), 52, 67; Getty Images: 11, 50, 56, 64, 70 (Bettmann), 33 (Corbis Historical),
73 (Mara Vivat), 14 (Walter Sanders/The LIFE Picture Collection); Helen Keller
International: 75; Library of Congress: 12 (Bain Collection), cover, back cover, 2, 15 top
and 15 bottom, 32, 38, 39; National Portrait Gallery: 29; Perkins School for the Blind:
1, 8, 16, 17, 18, 25, 57; Washington National Cathedral: 74.

Index